Nottinghamshii

on old picture p

Angela Franks

Summit Colliery, East Kirkby.

1. East Kirkby - Summit Colliery, so named because it stood at the highest point between Mansfield and Pinxton. Sinking started in 1887 and it became one of the largest pits in the country. In 1966 Summit colliery produced over one million tons. Whenever targets were reached, the Union Jack was flown. Summit closed in 1969.

Designed and published by
Reflections of a Bygone Age,
Keyworth, Nottingham 2000

Printed by Adlard Print
& Reprographics Ltd

£3.50

Introduction

Before the First World War, enthusiasm among the working classes for sending and collecting picture postcards had become almost a national obsession. You could post a card in the morning, making an arrangement to meet that evening, and know it would be delivered in time, all for the sum of one halfpenny. Photographers, some anonymous, and others working for well-known local publishers such as Ellis of Mansfield, travelled widely to record everything from the grand and ancient to the terraced houses and workplaces of ordinary folk.

At the same time, coal production from Britain's 3,024 mines was at its peak. Nottinghamshire coal mines stretched the length of the county and in Eastwood alone 40% of the workforce were employed down the pits which dominated the skyline with their stacks, headstocks and growing spoiltips, and made intriguing subjects for postcard photographers. It is fitting, then, that the story of coal mining in Nottinghamshire can be told through the medium of old picture postcards. Many of the cards in this book date from before 1918 and, as all trace of the once powerful coal mining industry rapidly disappears from the county, they provide a unique record of the mining communities of Nottinghamshire.

The county's association with coal, though at its height in the 150 years of the Industrial Revolution, stretches back centuries. Coal from the exposed seam on the western edge of the county was comparatively easy to obtain using primitive methods. Traces of bell pits still remain in areas such as Strelley where, as at Cossall, Selston and Wollaton, coal was mined in the Middle Ages. But it was during the wood famine of the 16th century that fortunes were made, so that by 1588 Sir Francis Willoughby was able to finance the building of Wollaton Hall from the wealth created by coal mining. But even though demand continued to grow, several developments had to take place before Nottinghamshire could benefit. The first came in 1712, when Thomas Newcomen's steam engine was designed to pump water out of mines. By the end of the eighteenth century, engines based on Newcomen's invention were also used for winding. Mining and steam power were to be linked for over two centuries. The problem of poor roads was addressed when colliery owners encouraged the building of the Erewash Canal in 1779 and the Nottingham Canal in 1796. Railways soon followed, and again it was coalowners like Barber and Walker who were instrumental in setting up the Midland Counties Railway which opened in 1839. It was now possible to move eastwards across the county and exploit the concealed coal seam; the first one with the foresight to do this was Thomas North in 1843 at Cinderhill (Babbington).

Sinking shafts in the concealed seam proved a costly and lengthy business. In 1922, because of debts of £500,000, the Harworth Main Colliery Company were forced to abandon the sinking of Harworth and hand over to the Barber Walker Co.; even in 1868, Thomas North died over £190,000 in debt. Also, the new pits were much deeper, and as the business of mining became more complex, the pit tops covered many acres with a network of railway lines, taller headstocks and associated industries such as brick or iron works alongside, all dwarfed by the spoil tips. The number and variety of trades needed for the efficient operation of a mine increased so that bricklayers, blacksmiths, engineers, and, later, electricians became indispensable.

Coal soon earned its nickname of 'black gold' for it was the raw material which fuelled the heavy industries and transport essential to the wealth and power of the British Empire. Evidence of this wealth was all too apparent in Nottinghamshire, where a list of the great houses in the county corresponds closely with those whose fortunes came from coal, from Sir Robert Clifton at Clifton Hall to the Seely family at Sherwood Lodge, northwards to the Duke of Portland at Welbeck Abbey. Meanwhile, the lot of ordinary miners was wretched. They worked in barbaric conditions and lived in poverty.

Miners organised themselves into unions and took action to improve pay and working conditions, though their early struggles seemed in vain because the private owners quickly broke agreements. So there was great optimism when nationalisation took place in 1947. During the 1950's and 60's long needed improvements and modernisation took place at pits right across the county. In the 1950's, 35,000 men worked in the coalfields of North and South Nottinghamshire. But the opening up of the oilfields spelled the end of coal's reign as the major source of fuel. After a brief resurgence in the 1970's and a great deal of industrial unrest in the 1980's, pit closures increased from a trickle to a flood. By January 2000, Nottinghamshire pits were once again privately owned, and only four remained open: Clipstone, Welbeck, Thoresby and Harworth. Between them they employed 1,174 men and their combined output was 198,842 tons.

Ex-miners have retrained and taken up a wide range of different jobs from nursing to hotelkeeping. They do not miss working underground, but they do regret the loss of the camaraderie and community spirit for which they were famous. They have a fund of stories about working down the pit and are proud to have been part of a once vital industry.

Angela Franks
September 2000

2. **Harworth Colliery** is the headquarters of RJB Mining. The Northern Union Mining Company, backed by German capital, first planned to sink the mine just before World War 1. The original name, Stinsdorf, had to be changed because of anti-German feeling. At the outbreak of war, the 16 German workers were interned and the property confiscated. Published by Scrivens of Doncaster, this card was posted from Bawtry on August 10th 1925.

Acknowledgments

My grateful thanks to the following for their help in researching this book: **Rachel Harrison**, Senior Clerical Officer, the Coal Authority; **Anne Howatson**, Senior Library assistant, Bircotes Library; **Joanne Stewardson**, Assistant Curator, the National Coal Mining Museum for England, for dates and other statistics about Nottinghamshire mines; **Mick Noble**, Deputy Superintendent, the Mines Rescue Station, for up to date information about the brigade, and for the loan of cards; **Brian Turner**, who from 1951 to 1987 worked at Newstead, Kirkby and Bentinck, and **Graham Wheeldon**, who between 1968 and 1988 worked at Bentinck, Langton and Summit (with so many years service in the mines, Graham and Brian provided useful insights into life underground); **Frank Smith** of Pinxton, for the story of John King's Patent; **David Ottewell** and **Peter Cooke** for the loan of postcards; and my husband, **Greg Franks**, for all his support and for his work on the map.

3. Annesley Pit near Kirkby in Ashfield was sunk in 1890. By 1982 the Annesley Bentinck Concentration Scheme was completed, but the pit closed in January 2000. Methane gas emissions from Bentinck will be used to supply heating to 15,000 houses. This H.G.Owston of Annesley Woodhouse card was posted in August 1909.

4. The extensive system of railway lines and piles of pitprops catch the eye in this view of **Mansfield Colliery.** At one time, hundreds of trains carried coal to all parts of the country from the coalfields. The wooden pitprops were sometimes referred to as the 'miners' friend' because their creaking alerted the men to an imminent roof fall.

5. Owned by the New Hucknall Company, **Bentinck (Kirkby)**, also the family name of the Dukes of Portland, started production in 1896. It was the first British colliery to produce one million tons in seven months, and in 1978, 20 acres of barley was grown on the tip. The card was postally used at Kirkby on August 25th 1911.

6. By the 1980s these screening sheds at **Bentinck** were part of a modern coal preparation plant which also processed coal from Annesley and Newstead. Most of the output went to Ratcliffe Power Station. In April 2000 the winding wheels were purchased for £100 and taken to a mining heritage centre at Newcastle under Lyme.

7. A Barber Walker colliery near Eastwood, **Brinsley** (1872-1970) was where D. H. Lawrence's father worked. From six in the morning till four in the afternoon he crouched in an 18-inch coal seam. Now you can picnic beneath the headstocks, approaching them via a path which was the route of the railway line from the pit to Langley Mill.

8. Digby near Eastwood is notable for what happened during the General Strike. In the autumn of 1926, 70% of the men at Digby had resumed work and the rest begged George Spencer (Labour MP and NUM official) to get their jobs back. For this he was expelled from the union and the breakaway Spencer union was formed.

9. Babbington Colliery No1 Rescue Team (c.1911) on one of their training days at Mansfield Woodhouse Rescue Station. By 1911 each colliery had to have a part-time rescue team to cover each shift. The station superintendent is there in uniform and the dog sometimes accompanied the Brigade on emergency calls.

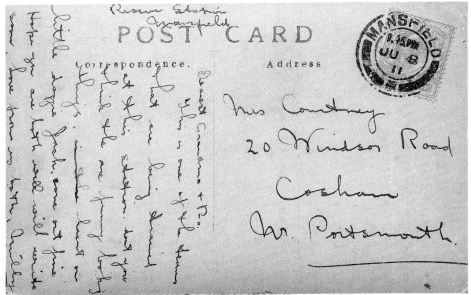

10. Reverse of the above. The card, sent from the training station on June 8th 1911 and postmarked Mansfield, reads: *"Dearest Grandma and Pa, This is one of the teams that are being trained at this station. Don't you think they are funny looking things. Hasn't our little doggie Jack come out fine.......Milly"*

11. Cinderhill - Babbington (Basford), sunk between 1841 and 1843, was the first pit in the Notts concealed coal seam. It was developed by Thomas North, a legend in his own lifetime, and a pioneer who introduced much new technology including the tandem-linked headgear which can be seen in the picture. He also built 28 miles of private railway line. When North died, penniless, it was the miners who

CINDERHILL

contributed to his memorial which still stands in Old Basford cemetery. The man with the horse and cart is going to the landsales office and the trucks are Midland Railway and Great Northern. After the pit closed in 1986, the Phoenix Business Centre was developed on the site. The card was postally used at Old Basford on January 2nd 1906.

12. Blidworth Colliery opened in 1926, and the village of Blidworth Vale was built to house the miners and their families. The colliery owners encouraged community spirit and the Manager was like a country squire, playing a leading part in village life. When transport improved, the practice of building pit villages died out.

I have visited Blidworth Colliery

13. This publicity card entitled *"I have visited Blidworth Colliery"* shows what a great change in attitude occurred after nationalisation in 1947. Throughout the 50s and 60s millions of pounds were spent on modernising above and below ground. Safety and environmental issues were of great importance.

14. Bilsthorpe Colliery, part of the North Notts Coalfield, was one of the many pits closed in the 1990s. Even though the Nottinghamshire Coalfield was regarded as comparatively safe, the closing years at Bilsthorpe were marked by tragedy when, in August 1993, three miners lost their lives as the result of a roof fall. (Rex Photo 874)

15. A postcard published by Judges of Hastings showing St. Wilfrid's Church, Wilford, with **Clifton Colliery** in the backgound. The steam and smoke which fill the skyline were a familiar feature of the Nottinghamshire landscape for over 150 years. When Clifton closed in 1960, it was still possible for men to gain employment at pits nearby.

16. Sir Robert Clifton sank the colliery at **Clifton** to pay off gambling debts. As landowner, he stood to make great profits from the leases and royalties the mine would produce. The pit and toll bridge across the Trent - replacing a ferry - were opened on June 16th 1870. 'Clumber' series colour postcard, posted on October 30th 1909.

THE CLIFTON COLLIERY PRIZE BAND.

17. Proud of their achievements, The **Clifton Colliery Prize Band** was typical of many which existed in the coalfields. Owners and management also encouraged other group activities such as football and cricket teams. Being a star of the team guaranteed a good job and favourable treatment during slack times.

18. The only Notts pit to be opened south of the Trent, **Cotgrave** started production in 1964 but was closed by 1992. Its clean modern lines contrast sharply with the clutter of the pre-nationalisation pit tops. Miners who worked at Cotgrave came from Scotland and the South East. The site is now a light engineering and business park.

19. Posted at Bulwell on April 28th 1909, the title **Hempshill Fan** refers to the lower stack, which is a furnace ventilation shaft chimney. This discharged foul air and gases from the upcast shaft. A further improvement occurred when radial flow fans made the atmosphere underground safe enough to install electric power & light.

20. A view of **Moorgreen** that explains why in *'Sons and Lovers'* D.H. Lawrence described it as set among cornfields while renaming it Minton. Nowadays the Black Shale Trail passes the area which was once the pit top. The Black Shale seam, 1000 feet below ground, was the deepest at Moorgreen and the last to be worked.

21. **Moorgreen Colliery** (1865 - 1985) was one of five pits owned by Barber Walker in the Eastwood area. In 1963, one million tons of coal was produced, but by 1985 the seams were exhausted. Today the site is called Colliers Wood and is part of the Eastwood Phoenix Project, a scheme set up to restore the woodlands.

22. This picture shows the primitive conditions in the screening sheds at **East Kirkby (Summit)**. Once on the surface, coal was transferred to the screens, rubble was removed and the coal graded before being loaded onto the waiting wagons. It was back-breaking and low paid work, given to older or disabled miners and boys.

23. Especially noticeable in this picture of **East Kirkby (Summit)** is the number of children employed. From 1870, school was compulsory up to 13 years of age but loopholes meant that many left at 12. In 1900, only 1 in 70 children had secondary education. In 1908, boys earned between 1s 8d (9p) and 1s 5p (7p) per day.

24. The miners are coming off shift at **Hucknall No 2 Colliery**. Their flat caps were thickly padded but gave little protection. On the right a full tub has emerged from the cage and been loaded onto a tipper (or tippler). This will revolve allowing the tub to shed its load onto the conveyor belt in the screening shed. The miners are carrying cans of drink for 'snap' time (mealbreak). They wanted 'snap' to be part

HUCKNALL N&2 COLLIERY

of the shift, but the managers disagreed, and it became a source of friction. In 1957, rebuilding at Hucknall no. 2 included reinforced concrete headstocks and even an office for the union rep. who, in the early days, had to loiter in the lamproom between shifts.

25. This postcard of **New Hucknall Collieries**, Huthwaite, shows a busy day at the pit. The enormous spoil tips nearby gave off sulphurous fumes and lit up the night sky. The pit, sunk in 1876, was a gassy mine and in 1983 up to 100 million litres of pure methane were drawn off each week. The area is now a golf course.

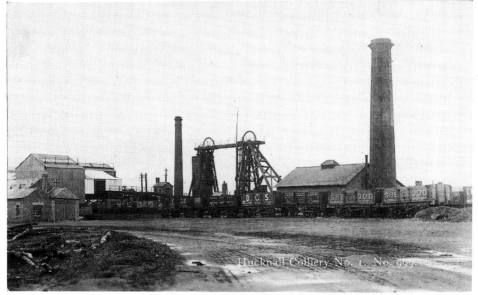

26. Hucknall Colliery No.1 on a card published by C. and A.G. Lewis of Nottingham in the 'Robin Hood Brand' series. Sunk in 1851 by J. E. Ellis, this was the first deep sinking in the Leen Valley. In 1955, serious subsidence occurred and the whole of Belvoir Street in Hucknall was wrecked. Between 1957 and 1969 the colliery was modernised.

27. Opened in 1852 by Barber Fletcher Company, **Kimberley** was in the exposed coal seam in the west of the county. The mine was on land owned by Lord Stamford and ceased production in 1897. The wooden headstocks and windlass at the entrance to the shaft show the rough and ready conditions in many Victorian mines.

28. This card of **coal-picking at East Kirkby** during the 1912 strike, which started on March 1st, was published by Henfrey of Kirkby. It shows how quickly local photographers reacted to the various crises in the coal mining industry. A million men were involved in this dispute, which lasted until mid-April and was over rates of pay - miners were paid by tonnage of coal produced, a system unfair to those working in difficult seams. During the strike, life soon became a struggle, with only a few shillings income from the union, so miners resorted to the illegal practice of coal picking. Sometimes mine owners sent in the constabulary to stop it. A compromise was achieved, but the struggle over pay continued for decades.

29. The Brickworks at **Harworth Colliery** were established by the German developers. Barber Walker took over in 1922 and planned to use the bricks to build the colliery village of Bircotes, but their poor quality led to the closure of the brickworks, and Watnall bricks were used. This card was posted in August 1916.

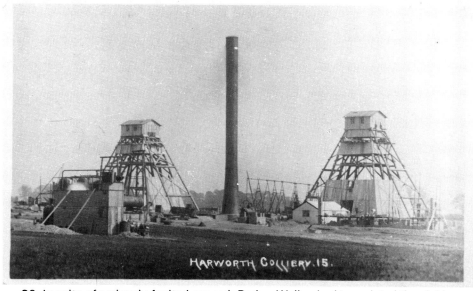

30. In spite of seriously faulted ground, Barber Walker had completed the sinking (shown here) of two shafts at **Harworth** by December 1923. The excellent coal was used by the *Flying Scotsman* on her record-breaking run from London to Edinburgh in 1932, a record later broken by the *Silver Jubilee*, also burning Harworth coal.

TROWELL COLLIERY, STAPLEFORD, NOTTS.

31. Trowell Colliery, Stapleford Notts, (1881-1928). A railway line was opened from Nottingham to Trowell in 1875, and the full coal trucks on the left are just leaving the pit. Trowell Field, an earlier Trowell pit was, in 1773, one of the first in the area to use a steam engine for pumping instead of soughs (drainage channels).

32. Mansfield Colliery Rescue Team No3 (c.1911) in Meco breathing apparatus, and with a canary. In the 1980s the colliery had an aviary of 22, while the rescue station had 18. As the birds warned of carbon monoxide gas, two accompanied the team on each call out, and were only replaced by electronic detectors in the 1990s.

33. Crown Farm Colliery, Mansfield (4353), Forest Town and Mansfield Colliery are all names for the same colliery and show the problem faced by postcard collectors when trying to locate various pits. Rival postcard publishers would often produce a number of views of a well-known pit taken from slightly different angles.

34. Mansfield Colliery, Forest Town, opened in 1906 by the Bolsover Company. The suburb of Forest Town was built for the mining community. All that remains of the old colliery, now a business park, is two half winding wheels set in concrete and landscaped spoil tips. Clipstone Colliery headstocks, Europe's tallest, are nearby. The postcard was published by S. Osler of Forest Town Post Office

VICTOR

BRITON

UNDERGROUND STABLES
MANSFIELD COLLIERY

35. The **Underground Stables, Mansfield Colliery**, look brightly-lit and well maintained. The job of handler was sometimes passed down through generations of the same family, and the Pit Ponies Protection Society ensured the animals were well cared for. Ponies were introduced in 1824 to replace female labour and at one time there were 70,000 in British pits, but by 1971 all had left the mines. Miners often gave the ponies treats, including a good pinch of snuff.

36. Early rescue work was left to volunteers like the St John's Ambulance Brigade which miners were encouraged to join. In 1906 the Permanent Corps Rescue Brigade was set up, and by 1912 became compulsory. **The Miner's Rescue Station** opened in Mansfield Woodhouse in 1909 and moved to Leeming Lane in 1958.

37. The first brigades were similar to the fire brigade and, usually, ex-military men were officers. Mansfield Woodhouse station superintendent J.G. Huskisson stands by a Standard motor car c. 1912. The cost of the station was met by the local mine owners. Today most of the £4.5 million expenses are covered by RJB Mining.

38. The use of breathing apparatus is being demonstrated at the old York Street premises of the **Rescue Station** which had only a small training gallery, in contrast to the 500ft of realistic underground roadways beneath Leeming Lane. The old equipment was both cumbersome and heavy. The modern version, known as S. E. F. A. (Self Elevated Flow Apparatus), is made of stainless steel with a spun alloy cylinder which makes it much lighter. It is worn on the back rather than the chest.

OAKES COLLIERY C?
N°I RESCUE TEAM ·

39. After 1911 each pit had several rescue teams, and training them was a major part of the brigade's work. In the picture, the men of **No.1 Rescue Team** are waiting to enter a smoke-filled gallery. Most mining accidents have one of three causes: explosion, roof fall or inrush, so rescuers are trained to meet hazardous situations in enclosed conditions where it is possible to work for only about 45 minutes. It is years of such expertise that is nowadays sought after by private companies.

40. Teams taking part in exercises in the old underground gallery at **Mansfield Woodhouse.** In the new premises, realistic conditions could be created when in a few minutes the roadways could be filled with smoke and the temperature and humidity increased. Present members of the brigade must have worked for two years underground and have regular fitness checks. No safety helmets are being worn in the picture, but today the brigade wear green, and ordinary miners wear yellow.

41. Underground photographs, such as this one of a junction at the **Pit Bottom, Summit Colliery, Kirkby**, are quite rare. This was published about 1912 by A. W. Lane of East Kirkby. The tubs on the left are empty and on their way back down the road to the coal face. The young lad (ganger) holds a hook which attached the tub to a chain so that it could be hauled up an incline before descending through gravity deeper into the mine. On the right, tubs are waiting to ascend in the cage (chair) while full tubs are being loaded. To save the long walk to the coal face, miners are having a lift in the empty tubs. The floor of the mine would be littered with crushed tins which had contained snuff, used by the miners in place of cigarettes. Note the absence of any protective clothing, which was not introduced until the 1930's.

RUFFORD COLLIERY N⁰ MANSFIELD 'Ellis

42. This Ellis postcard shows **Rufford Colliery** near Mansfield in full production. The mine was first owned by the Bolsover Company, the third largest colliery company in the country. The building in the centre houses the winding engine which was kept in immaculate condition by the highly skilled winders.

RUFFORD COLLIERY

43. These temporary wooden headstocks were erected during the sinking of **Rufford Colliery** between 1911 and 1913. Disaster struck In February 1913, when a seven ton steel water barrel plunged 115ft into the workings. Fourteen men lost their lives and four escaped by clinging onto debris in the icy water. Most shafts of this period were round and bricklined, though metal tubbing was also used. Modern ones are usually lined with concrete.

44. Opened in 1874 by the Newstead Colliery Company, **Newstead Colliery** ceased production by 1984. The High Main Seam was only 80 feet below ground and miners could hear the trains rumbling overhead, even being able to distinguish passenger from goods trains. The colliery was surrounded by railway lines, with the LMS on the western side and the GCR on the east alongside the Annesley

sheds. In 1963, when the line was closed as a result of the Beeching axe, miners filled the LMS tunnel to Newstead village with spoil from Bentinck, only for it all to be removed in the 1980's in preparation for the Robin Hood Line. The railway in the foreground is now part of that line, which was so named because it runs through the Robin Hood hills.

RUFFORD COLLIERY

45. Pithead baths were built at **Rufford Colliery** in 1941, and it was further improved during the 1950s with modern headstocks and surface buildings. Underground, no.2 shaft was deepened to 738 metres, and no.3 shaft to a depth of 803 metres at a cost of millions of pounds. Rufford closed in 1993.

46. Policemen at **Newstead**, possibly during the 1926 Strike and Lockout. Apart from one ordinary constable, the rest are officers, and the seated gentleman looks important enough to be a commissioner. Constables would have been brought in by the management to guard the mine during the strike.

47. Members of staff at **Newstead** pose for a photograph. The three wearing watch chains and collar and tie are obviously important, while the gentleman in the bowler hat could even be the manager. The group probably also includes an engineer and electrician. There were sidings at Newstead for both North Eastern and Midlands railways.

NEW OLLERTON COLLIERY.

48. The Butterley Company development at **New Ollerton** included a factory providing employment for the miners' families and a model village supervised by 'Butterley Constables'. Failure to conform could result in swift eviction and job loss. The card was posted on September 20th 1938.

SHIREBROOK COLLIERY.

Sprittlehouse, Photo., Alfreton. (Copyright.)

49. **Shirebrook**, on the Derbys/Notts border, opened in 1896, merged with Pleasley in 1984 and closed in 1993. The waste in the foreground is typical of early pit tops when owners were reluctant to pay anyone to remove rubble. Shirebrook is now a business park and the Robin Hood Line runs nearby. The card was posted in 1908.

Shirebrook Colliery

50. Published by Ruddock of Lincoln, this card posted from Shirebrook in August 1919 reads : *"We have just come up from this coalmine. I wish you could have seen us crouching along with our miner's lamps 1800 ft below ground. I am glad we had the chance to go down as it is quite difficult to get permission. . . Love Gwen."*

WARSOP MAIN COLLIERY.

51. Warsop Main Colliery (Staveley Coal and Iron Company) opened in 1890. The asterisk marks the shaft that Alf went down. The message reads: *"Six of us went a tour down this pit this afternoon.... We were down three hours.......It is 600ft deep, it was a unique experience."* This postcard was sent from Shirebrook in May 1911.

52. Sunk in the 1770s, **Wollaton** was one of the last pits to send coal via the Nottingham Canal (opened 1796) which had 21 locks, including a flight of 14 at Wollaton. Canals were a cheap and efficient means of moving bulky cargo. Wollaton and Radford merged in 1961, but both are now closed. The card was published by Stapleford photographer Marrin.

53. Between 1902 and 1903 two shafts were sunk at **Sherwood** by Sherwood Colliery Company. Pits in the concealed seam were large and had great impact on the countryside. By 1934, Sherwood had pit head baths, and in 1983 both winders were electrified. Production had ceased by 1992. This card was posted in 1906.

54. Sent to West Cowes in 1912, the year of a coal strike. The message reads: *"This p.c. shows the last colliers to leave the Sherwood Colliery Company Pit at Mansfield Woodhouse ... things are very quiet so far but they may be very much to the reverse before long, for I see no prospect of a settlement at present."*